Buttoned-up Shapes

George Tardios was Director of Totleigh Barton, the Arvon Foundation's first residential creative writing centre in Devon.

Has had poems in six 'PEN/Arts Council Anthologies' published by Hutchinson; the 'Puffin Book of Salt Sea Verse' edited by Charles Causley; 'The Way To Write', J. Moat & J. Fairfax (Elm Tree Books); 'English For Me', Eric Boagey (University Tutorial Press); 'Apple Fire', and 'On Common Ground', Jill Pirrie (Bloodaxe Books, and WWF).

A collection of poems, 'BullSong' was published by Charlotte Press. Recently, poems in 'Cadences' (European University of Cyprus), and 'The London Magazine'.

Participated in 'Poets in Schools' scheme and tutored creative writing courses for the Arvon Foundation.

Organised the first 'National Poetry Competition' for the Poetry Society at Earl's Court, and for the Arvon Foundation. Judged the BBC2 'South Bank Show' Poetry Competition.

Buttoned-up Shapes

Poems by George Tardios

For my mother Haji-Marie,
and her beloved and never-to-be-forgotten Island of Cyprus.

St Ursin Press

First published in Great Britain in 2015
by
St Ursin Press
3 Broadfield Court, 1-3 Broadfield Road, Folkestone,
Kent CT20 2JT, United Kingdom
www.trencavel.co.uk/st ursin.html

ISBN 978-09572485-6-4

St Ursin Press is an imprint of Trencavel Press

Contents

My Sad Spirits

My sad Spirits
Softly
Place their pains in line

Hang waiting memories
Like flaps of skin
To catch the wind.

My sad Spirits want their days to shine
Be better than they were before

They wish to pass along their line.

My sad Spirits sigh through mists
Struggle to still all stolen minds

Send desperate
Time-worn signs –

Swarms of buzzing grapes
Dizzy with demented bees

Oranges
Dipped in melted sun

Clouds of Starlings flex shape
Skid-on-air
Fall like tea-leaves
Into patient twigs

Twilight floods fields –
Underwater skeletons of coral trees
Land to sea.
A crack between the worlds

Stars
Broken stars
Shards of frozen glass
Shiver icing over curling leaves.

My Spirits sing

When we sense
Divinity in things –

Light on winter branches
Rushing skies breathed in

Exhaled
As spreading seed –
Poetry, art, angelic deeds.

Some
See no divinity at all

Ignore their dreams.

My sad Spirits softly
Place their pains in line

Hang waiting memories
Like flaps of skin
To catch the wind...

Alien Light

Lapithos.
In Lapithos
Light folds the sea in honey

Drowsy waves wash away the wedding feast.

Three days guzzling, guests crawl in sand like swine
Bulging suns burst at their eyes
Alien light
Ripens sleepers twinned in copper.

Distant
Shimmers of liquid glass
Break men in two.

Air lies like wine
Its drunken wafts wrap up the violins

Goats suckle at abandoned flutes
Gate-posts sprout shoots.

Even a priest, would take a wife in Lapithos.

Weighing down his donkey with his charm
Xenofos, 'catch' of the village, never caught
Danced a giant mirror on his knee.
Proudest of gifts, hugged safe.

Framed in flashing glass, Xenofos spun songs to still the birds
Through seasick fields and skies

Rode handsome from Morphou – 'Omorpho horko'
To be best man in Lapithos.

Lapithos – white tables lined the shore
The mirror was set in sand against the tide.

Balancing a twisted handkerchief, matching palms
The groom and best man danced the bride

A fickle rush of cloud teasing the sea.

Mouthing the moon, Xenofos made songs for his friend the groom
Keeper of mad men in Lapithos.

The fiddler stitched them tight.

No one knew how, perhaps the wine had sipped their sight
Third wedding dawn, repeated in the glass
They found the best man with the bride.

Tied backwards to his donkey, drunk
They whipped him home – one week over Kyrenia's rocks.

The donkey died. Xenofos sang on
Seeing her face daily born in sharp and shining things.

He wept over puddles, wells, cuts from broken glass
Soaking in *his* bride.

The strange light in his name slipped inside his head.

Ashamed, the father turned his picture to the wall, hung glass in black
Gave him away, to the only place for lunatics he knew

In Lapithos.

Prickly Pears

Prickly pears suited Christos
He too sucked his years from dead ground.

Parents nameless
Nourished by priests –
Who planted Christ in his name
Picked him a wormy wife –
He carried God on his shoulders
Worshipped the scorching air

A sparse-bearded, black-bible man
Riddled with prayer.

His house slept six dowryless daughters
Nothing more

Even when passing barefoot, the tail of his vrakka swaggered
And swept his steps clear.

But cactus crowded his land.

In the cool before sunrise, treading thorns
He fished for fruits with split bamboo.
Balanced in brown paper
Carved into liquid coals.

He stood with the sun at noon
Beside his handcart, selling for two piastres:
"Siga...Baboutso-siga..."

He burned.
His fruit bathed in a pail.

Life stretched –
Until the night the cutting wind slid down the mountains
Scythed his cactus clean.

Stung in sleep
Shrieking thorns slammed against glass
Christos stuttered naked into the storm

His mouth vinegar
Teeth clenched skulls

Torrents baptised the barrels of his gun

His forefinger crossed the trigger.

He aimed his soul at some point
Only Christos saw

The twelve-bore
Boomed through God.

The Schoolmaster

Son of a shepherd
Yiorgos saw further than his barren village
His father's cob-webbed eyes –
Education irrigated the land.

In the school-less village no one could think
Of chalking themselves snail-like onto slate.
Soon as they walked, they worked
Made brittle by drought, at the mercy of what they knew.

Once a year only, a river slipped through.

Though his name marked him a cultivator
Tiller of lands
He chose to seed sleeping minds.
Studying while friends slept
Wanting to know more, the more he knew.
Kerosene-lit knowledge flickered into his eyes
Fermenting in lamp-musk
Until moths drummed in his brain.

Dawn
Father found him among cold ink-clots, oil spent
Hand curving the hip of lamp-glass.

Immersed in goats
The father was led by his son.

Scholarships wrenched Yiorgos free
Onto the camel-caravan for Nicosia town

Mired in a rushing bazaar where nothing grew –
Donkey-carts, beating brass
Liquid-backed water sellers –
He nurtured a meagre moustache to fill his face
The window-vegetables in the blind widow's house.
Cleaned and cooked for bed and board
Became a schoolmaster.

Winter
Steaming with father's herds
Moulded mud and straw into a one-room school
Free for the poor.
Others could pay in goat-cheese, cracked-olives, okes of beans.

No one came.
With no sounds to support, it crumbled silently.

Yiorgos' bamboo-cane parted fields
Winnowed children from family crops, grazing beasts, parents' wrath.
Deeply rooted, Yiorgos argued
Even fought.
His prize – more minds in school.

The classroom ballooned with voice
Somersaulted ideas like spores
Dammed the yearly river flow
Ripened village fields.

People muttered –
"Where the schoolmaster treads, the earth trembles."

Yiorgos picked (as expected) a vulnerable wife –
Swollen Eleni, village discard
"Raped," she wept. Pleaded protection.
Without male strength her child would spoil.

Yiorgos opened the door
Planted his name on her son.
Seeded one of his own.

Father tipped his hat
To the schoolmaster's wife –
Felt the sinking weight of his heart.

Both sons grown
Blown to foreign lands
Eleni reads him letters.
His light is lost.
Long study with parched lamps was to blame.
Books and beasts lie fallow.

Sleeps in sun he cannot see
Awoken by leaves of air against his cheek –
"Eleni? Eleni-mou? Is there a guest?"
"No, my husband. Just me."
She damps him down in his straw seat.

He knows

He knows
True knowledge can strike you blind.
Men cross his door in sheaves

"Eleni?"
"No one, my husband.
Just me."

Evil Eyes

In fractured mountains
Her white wedding united guests in smiles
Pinned best-men and bridesmaids with carnations.
Lined either side at the altar
They pledged themselves.
Signed silk-ribbons held them together.

Her widowed mother, kneeling
Crossed herself
Felt relief through her knees

With God's help, the broker and the orange groves
Her cracked daughter, 'the dribbling one' was joined

"And to such a man."
Odysseus, the village catch
Invader of womens' dreams

A hollow horse.

The bargain bent the daughter's neck
Fearful of female stares
Their Siren chills.

The fiddler sawed them home sealed in a line
Past mocking blinds and gnawing eyes.
With incense at the head –
(burnt olive-leaves clears bad blood from the brain)
The priest swung at each tortured house
Smoking out the musk.

In muzzled heat
Torments of daughters turned mothers green.

"A ripe olive for a prune" they sang, eyes like nails
"The dowry dragged him in."

Street oil-drum dammed, the feast began,
Ouzo to milk the sight, bouzouki to skewer the heart.
House-door broached like a Han –
Their twin photographs and haloed wedding wreaths
Were hung in a wooden heart
Locking them in glass above the marriage bed.

Reflected in the heart
The village danced
Down on their heads.

Silent, unlike his ancient name
Odysseus, already in amongst the fat
Waited his chance

The hot-cockerel clicking of his hands
Trotting grunt as his heels stamped
Snatched up his bride
Made his own dance for the money.
Pocked with licked pins, bristling notes
Spilt red wine on her dress
A spreading blot.
Only cicadas heard the stumbled passage to their bed.

In the painful morning her mother roused them
Hung the white sheet for the village to see.

Yawning with the stretching sun
Matriarchs welcomed this defeated flag
Unmarked.
They and daughters howled for honour.

Singed by shame
Tongue melting to her mouth
The mother spooned her shaking daughter close
Like a lamb newborn to winter wind.
Wailing to heaven both collapsed to their knees.

There was no male kin
So the mother slit her silent in the square
Clotting the dribbling one in dust
Beside the salt stain of her virgin tears.

The groom too drunk
Had snored like Cyclops through the night.

The mother kept her in the heart
Celibate for seven years,
Then like charred paper fell apart.

Collecting water for his fields one night
Odysseus drowned.

Above the unspoiled marriage bed
Heart-hinged glass.
A single eye blind with dust
Binds the bride together –

Two wedding wreaths
And signed silk-ribbons.

Petros

Aged Petros
And the mud wall
Supported each other.

Then
Heartcaught
By the log fire
Petros grew colder
Wood outlived rock.

Heartbeats ago
Limbs jerked
For nourishment.

They found him
Crumbling.
His glass of tea sat by
His side
Still breathing.

Outside
Mud dusted the ditch.

The Hermit

In the village kafenion
Where men arguing politics
Held newspapers upside down
Most agreed (a rare event) that
Ungrateful Theodoros – 'gift from God'
Had thrown away his name
His will to live this given life.

Abandoned infant at church door
Adopted by the ancient priest
Theodoros – while in the womb, before the name –
Already knew his welcome cries would wake
The priest's remaining doldrum days.
And though he considered it nonsense
Ensured his own baptism (before the devil could appear)
In shrieking ice-water of the one true faith.

Church-goers believed
The thumbed-cross oiled on his forehead, first utterance of his name
Sparked his soul to life, within its human frame.

Theodoros smiled; his purpose chosen outside this world.

The bow-legged Father, emaciated by hunger
The only holy-man for miles, now happily stretched his time.
Early morning, milked the stale-urine stench of goats into his tea
The child's glass bottle.
Ensured the brown-rubber nipple of dummy was dipped in honey
Before he stumbled over hills, infant tied to his back, preaching
"We make our own worlds – nothing exists, until given a name."

In this rock-strewn village, hidden away from enviable towns
Most struggled to feed their own.
They resented collection-money spent
Weaning an unwanted child –
"Should be left on a rock for eagles."

Families cooked secretly, locked against begging neighbours
Bolted their food.
Except the Father
Heart wide as his stance, who gave away all he owned.
"Except the goats – kept for straddling," some joked.

The priest, Father Nikiforos, despite his strenuous treks
The only father Theodoros knew
Died when he was five.

To Theodoros, he was still alive.

Out of guilt
Theodoros was slipped through reluctant households, like a bar of soap
Made to work in fields, herd goats –
He somehow grew, only to shrink away.
Among the mountain pines dreamt for hours
Overheard to converse with shadows.
Wanted nothing from this life.
No point to see the world
It thrived inside his head.

He would say to passers by, *"We deflect ourselves.*
To pursue happiness is an empty road!
More profitable to seek oneself instead."

Found a cave in a cliff, hacked out rooms.
Lived on wild-chestnuts, olives, mountain greens
For more years than the span of man.

And when, gratefully, he slipped to other worlds
Only youngsters could remember
An ethereal presence that barely spoke
Wanted only to perceive the air.

They found his paintings on cave walls

His hand moved by Spirit
To freeze moments of time
Illuminate lives.
A reminder to truly see

Olives big as boulders, flaming with oil
Like liquid eyes upon them.

Leaf-bursting trees crying out
The years they had known.

Sawing cicadas
Chuckling magpies
The pee-wit whistle of hawks.

A lone goat, searching at the edge of a cliff
Overlooking the sea.

Glowing butterflies
Flying colours around the walls...

In the muffled cave
They listened to their own heartbeats flapping
Melting.

At night, each image changed their dreams.

Revisiting the cave, they began again to feel

Themselves.

The cave became a shrine.
Its paintings drew pilgrims from foreign lands

And villagers tended them
As a gift from God.

Ourania

Her eyes were not blue as her name
'Ourania' – liquid sky
A rushing thickness, she never heard

Though blue was the apron she shamelessly chose
Over black
To show she had *not* been a widow.

With child, but no husband
Forced, or willing, no one knew

No man would have her.

Her father, brother, beat her deaf.
The village showed its back.

Outcast by sin, she begged in silence
Nightly baked bread to sell
Worked alongside roadgang men.

She paid all she had to educate her son
In a life without light, the one bright star –
Hard enough for normal folk.

Under a thirsty sun her apron gathered grime
Her curves drooped dry as carob fruit.
Invisible amongst the men
Shovel in hand
Toothless, walnut-faced –
The village passed her by
Forgetting
The most crushed carob yields the sweetest juice.

Unused to kind words this cloudless soul
Would gape a doorway of a smile
Invent a flood of gifts, give up her life for casual friends.

With time
Ashamed
Her star left home, abandoning his choking past
The drowning blue
For concrete European skies.

She lost her sight (extinguished by his missing light)
Heavy work, villagers said, could burst the blood

Sat till the end on broken chair
Outside her hut at village edge
Smiling
Sucking water-melon chunks
Glugging coarse red wine.

Her neighbours secretely brought food.

Her son never wrote
Never returned.

Ioulia and Francos

i.
Meeting eyes across ripe melons
In Nicosia market
Unmade them

Ioulia, unstained by sun
Wearing wide-hats with veils
Town born, attended by maids
Discovered she drained blood from his veins

To her own thighs, stirring.

Thwarting parents' wishes, father's final slap
She married Francos.

"A village shopkeeper?"

A magazine-handsome, import-export
Morphou man.

Disowned by family, she leapt into his heart
Moved to a mud-house village
Gave away her hats.

In no man's land –
Goats, hens, pigeons
Barefoot, burnt-faced neighbours
Herded through their home.

It was custom
To leave front doors unlocked.

Like frontier guards they watched her
Kneeling at their feet
Open her cedar wedding chest
Offer handwoven sheets, Lefkara spidered-crochet
Silk pillow slips, rare scent
Passing to the ferryman
Until her Pandora's box was spent.

The border safely crossed.

Having sat on scissors sure-sign of a girl
Ioulia hid a secret Icon under the mattress.
Saint Mamas would protect her bed
Send down a son.

A daughter came instead.

ii.
Francos –
Inheriting parents' store
A silent shop-bell
Mouldy sacks of crumbled beans housing ants for free
Toasted newspapers, a dry Bible –
Taught himself to see between the lines.
Stretched trade abroad
Made the shop ring.

In the daily Kafenion
Older men, unable to read
Watched his words.

Taking wife and daughter on the Christian Haj
Hung a halo over their heads

Baptism in Jordan River
Renamed them –
Haji-Francos
Haji-Oulia
Haji-Marie

But no boys were born.

Miscarriages cost them dear

Each time
Doctors swelled like ticks
The shop pulled in its head.

Two more daughters.
Cursed with daughters.

iii.
Having milked the morning goats for cheese
Haji-Oulia, headscarfed and aproned
Sold from her market-stool, loom-woven cloth

Lengthening lines on her cheeks.

Wearing waistcoated suits in his sun-pierced shop
More dust-motes than goods outnumbering flies
Haji-Francos unexpectedly folded
Like a Muslim
Forehead kissing the floor.

Cockroaches steered around his form.

Unsealing himself, stumbled home
At height of noon, sun-fevered
Slipping through shadows.

Told his wife
Archangel Michael, collector of souls
Had slapped him down.
He'd be dead by 4 after noon

And to fetch the priest.

Haji-Oulia arguing
Three daughters weeping
He lay down
Waiting for the priest to call.

The doctor was an after-thought

Who found
No ill
Except a burning handprint on one cheek.

Haji-Francos was not yet thirty-two.

iv
Haji-Oulia foresaw herself
Shrink in black, labouring in others' fields
Darkened by sun.
Nightly baking bread to sell.
Serving as maid.

Without dowries
Daughters would not make a match.

The Aunt would arrive by carriage
Offer piastres
Beg her return.

Instead, to feed the family
Haji-Oulia would sell the shop, preserve fruit
Post her favourite, Haji-Marie like a package
To working exile across the sea.

Thoughts collided
While Haji-Oulia held back the sun.

v.
Last rites taken
Haji-Francos predicted a future world
After final, earth-changing war
Ruled by *"little red men"*.
At 4 his breathing stopped.

The house exhaled.
Garden jasmine perfumed his corpse.
Flies flirted with church oil.
Figs fell.
Sobbing.
A donkey brayed.

Haji-Oulia hugged daughters tight
Moulding them
Into herself
Like dough.

Swollen River

Most fertile days
Tail of hazy summer

Swimming in pollen

Young Poli evaded school
Grazed neighbours' fields fed by the filling river
Devoured grapes, figs, carob, melons, nuts.

Despite meagre stores, stale bread, goat cheese
His father left in their empty shack
He thrived away from men.

Burrowed in woods as if tranced by Pan
Steaming through needling suns, nightly rains
Poli grew ripe, flyblown before his time.
A spreading plant without firm roots
Spilling disjointed feet, elastic arms
Limp shorts, a horny head.
His body drained vigour from his brain.

Elongated by sun thrown onto moving walls –
Cyclops in a shadow-play –
This flapping flag led classmates
Like seething ants around a defecating mule
Their gathered boldness infecting village peace at noon.

Unable to be best at school
He'd be the worst.

Woven together by smoking leaves
He danced with bees
Then smacked them flat.
Stole honey, uprooted shoots for fun
Made experimental love to goats

By the swollen river, taught followers how to blind cats –
Smothered their eyes with mud
Tied tin-cans to tails.
Gleefully set red ants against black
Turk fighting Greek, black always won.

Elders blamed his parents
Mother dead
Father in the hills with sheep
The boy had outgrown himself.
Left on his own, he'd pushed himself too soon.
Too soon into a man.

As locals foretold, he was expelled from school.
The whole village crossed to the other side.

In shaded doorways, holding up walls
All alone beneath a hammering sun
He began to feel cursed by his ancestral land
Leered at passers-by.

Hearing –
His father Stavros bore this cross
Like lambs he carried on his shoulders.
Poli was his only blood –
If he worked hard
In time… all would be well.

On a moon-touched night pitted with rain
Poli dragged kittens in a sack to drown

Over-stretched, he fumbled over roots, tripped
Was tugged down banks into a clawing rush
That filled his mouth with struggling fur.

Stavros finally left his sheep
Rushed to his son too late.
Waded into water howling
At the sky
The Gods
Himself

Swept away
Trying to gather the river in his arms.

The Miracle

The room was fixed
In underwater light.

Tranced villagers,
Planted like drop-mouthed stroke victims
Around her bed
Waited for the miracle.

Bony Hera, corkscrewed among sweaty sheets
Eyes stretched beyond the gloom
Opened her mouth.
The only thing to move
Uttering soundless words
To no one.

Trapped in withered legs since birth
Ignored by saints
Spilt on the bed, by a hunch-backed mother
Who accepted pain
She'd cursed and cursed the sainted church

Studying web-wrapped flies
Corner-caught on lime-washed walls.
Learning to tell time
From barred-window shadows binding her feet.

Until one night, her eighteenth year
Leaking a graveyard chill into the bed
Flooding her legs with blood
Hera began to pray in fear.

Summoned –
The Virgin touched her during sleep
Proclaimed –
For a boon she would heal before witnesses
Help her walk.
With the moon in flood
Hera should call the village to her room.

Scuttling down streets.
The black-widowed mother spun-out her news
Wrapped villagers in belief.

Mesmerised by miracles
They cocooned themselves in her oil-lit home.

The widow held herself up
On the iron frame, foot of the bed
Weaving between tall shadows.

No one heard
Hera speak
Saw what she saw

Only lips forming words
The sheets lift back, fold themselves
Hera's limpid body raised in air
Hung by a thread
Rotating.

"Holy Mother" people pleaded
"Holy Mother
Forgive us our sins"

Descending belly first
A thin red line
Drawn slowly down the spine.

Frenziedly they crossed
Themselves

Cupboard opening
Swathes of cotton-wool
Soaking up the swelling red.
Each swab, the Virgin's face
Dropped by the bed
Fading away.

The body turned itself.
Sheets tucked. Cupboard closed.
Unstained white cotton layered the floor.

Letting go, the mother crumbled
To her knees.

Hera begged all to leave.
Her sudden voice stung them alive.
Next day, she'd visit every home
But now, slipped within sleep's stickiest web.

Morning
Draped in a neighbour's smock, skipping through early sun
Hera kept well-away from shade.

Re-entering their daily work
"Another miracle" the people sighed
"Our offerings bring Saints close."

Hera kept her bond.
Devoted her body to Our Lady's Church
Shaved her head, lived in a cell
Standing always on the edge of darkness
Beside shuttered windows
The pulling moon.

Never seen to sit. Hardly ate.
Sipped chains of Turkish coffee.
Never slept.
Ever-treading barefoot psalms on flagstone floors.

In her cave-black home
Cloaked in threads thick as tar
The crouched mother mourned
The deserted bed

Her daughter flown.

So I'm Told

i.
Somewhere in Cyprus my legs still hang
So I'm told

Roof-dangling windchimes
Kicking against waxen body parts
Yellowed with incense
Tallow-smoke
Human dust
Repetitive prayers to Andreas the Apostle.

His Monastery, ancient finger-bone
Grips a peninsula tip slapped by sea
Holding fast its fame for miracles
Facing-off Mecca, the red-crescent sting of invading sun.

Every Saint's Day the yearly Fair
When all so named give gifts in celebration
There is a reckoning.
I am witness
So I'm told.

ii.
Autumn London, weeping weather.
Hooded, lost to sight
Forgotten streets unawakened by summer-light
Somers Town growls within its cave.

New shorts, first school, fenced playground
Encircled by raw, encrusted-nostril
Baboon-bum faces seeking prey.
A hobnailed kick between my legs
Freezes the day.

Wheelchair paralysed, medical mystery
Ordered repeatedly to cross myself
Mother wafts smoking olive-leaves around my lifeless legs.
Three months pass.

I'm told,
Registered money posted far away
Cyprus –
Photographed shaded-ladies fingering stitches
Caravanned camels
White moustaches dripped in coffee –
To black-dressed Gran baking at the outside oven
Moulds legs in bees-wax
Offerings to the Saint.

Pleading, my mother promises
Once healed I will visit Cyprus
Pilgrimage to the Monastery
All the island's holy shrines.
This, in place of sacrifice.

Week after my legs were hung, I walked.
A miracle
So I'm told.

Without funds, promises are blocks of stone.
I am five years old.

iii.
Two birthdays on, mother agreeing to Divorce
Her steaming settlement, thankfully separates us from London
Pounds us across a watery gap.
We're rattled through jig-saw countries
Even while we sleep.
I am eye-dumbfounded with rainbow adventures.

Unplugged from broody Naples
Alleys limp in washed linen
Vesuvios fat with fire belching stars at heaven
We float to the centre of the inland sea
Silently dragging darkness into docks at Limassol
Where unseen cicadas seek to answer the whale-song
Depth of stars.

Under this shivering light, earth exhales night-time heat.
Herbal warmth enfolds us both like wings
Pilgrims to a sun-scorched land asleep
In the middle sea of middle-earth –
Rancid goats, hiccuping donkeys, potent cocks
Beds laid on flat mud-roofs –
Pointing defiant finger at the Muslim coast.

Morning, street-sellers chant their wares.
An isle of wonders ripe with noises.

iv.
In the dusty market-square
My mother, 'Lady from London'
Hires drivers and two wooden-bodied buses
That shudder like chronic drunkards
Gasping asthmatic fumes
Fermented with invited villagers
Water melons, boiled eggs
Bubbling chickens.

Crucifixes, church-charms, talismen
Tremble from fractured mirrors.
Olives, sour bread, cheese
Knotted in sink-beaten handkerchiefs.

Shoeless peasants
Now stiff and shod in Sunday best.
Their lifetime opportunity to see the world.

Climbing like cautious flies
Prayers echo through Troodos mountains.
Spiralling road-shrines mark the dead
Mashed metal far below.
At every precipice we sing.

Off-road ride donkeys
Lie in holy hermits' caves
Body-worn hollows where they slept –
One size miraculously fits all
So I'm told –
Kiss glistening skulls
Browned bones
Polished by absolution-fevered mouths.

In churches, caught among believers
Sweat and smoke
We worship lipstick-blooded icons
Fingers pursed with holy water

Always crossing

And recrossing
Saints and miracles of old:
St. Chrisostomos – Golden-mouth
Stavrovouni – Crucifix Hill
St. Yennadios of Moronero – Cures colds (He was frozen to death)
St. Antipas – Toothache
St. Procopius – Boils
Panayia Aphendrika – Dispels the disease of any naked youth
who publicly smears himself with candle grease
Panayia Galatoussa – Renews milk in humans, and animals
St. Marina of Mesa Khorio – Calms nagging wives
St. George of the Black Hill – Reactivates broody hens
St. John the Baptist of Silikou – Heals malaria in children if they are
rolled up and down the aisle
The Virgin of Phaneromeni – Finds lost items, and suitable
sons-in-law (both Moslem and Christian)...

Days-end, off-loaded into mountain monasteries
Planked beds – Pilgrims' rights to three days stay with food –
We escape beard-growing monks' sweaty servings of clinging beans.

Outside, lit fires hole-punch the night
Perfume herb-stuffed goats, revolving chickens.
I listen to faces burnt with wine
Crackle tales of love denied.

Always crossing
And recrossing

Roadside pilgrims with their gifts
Astride donkeys or on foot the last three miles
Pulling strung goats and sheep.

I watch women fulfilling vows
Crawl to heaven on ravaged knees.
Doused from buckets, their sloughed bodies sweep stony ground
Flail like serpents frocked with hissing water
Gargling soured prayers.

v.
Until we reach
The panhandle tip on Fair's Day –
Palm-roofed stalls shade the sun
Dangle protective amulets
Tout chipped-ice with flavoured syrup.
Pastelli, deep fried dough-balls
Honeyed globes in paper cones
Salt-roasted chickpeas, pumpkin seeds, hemp.
Soujouko tentacles hung like saints.
Sweet silage smell of carob juice.

Shuffling in line down hill
Tapped-Spring by the sea
I obediently sip from mother's palm
Smokey miracle water
That once sprung beneath the Apostle's feet
Washed sight into a sea-captain's eyes.
Mother bathes my head – to aid intelligence.
And of course, my legs.

An air-trembling wail parts crowds…
Chewing on fear, I witness
Below monastery steps, an eroded widow
On red-soaked knees seeping into ancient stone
Babble to phantoms no one sees.
Each time she struggles onto steps
As if tossed high by giant hands
Is somersaulted backward, curled tight as an apple
Until she hits and bursts with wells of tears
Begging forgiveness of the empty air.

Heads bowed, the devout make signs of the cross, averting ill
Whisper, *"Each year are those who fail, attempt to cheat.*
Her lame son healed, she failed to keep her vows.
Last-minute thought to offer punished knees instead."

Eyes off the spreading sun
The Apostle showed his wrath at being denied
Blocked her entry to the monastery.
A miracle
So I'm told.

"He could if he so chose
Break humans across his knees like staffs."

Inside, crossing and recrossing in time to chanted psalms
Like sea-anemone in current
Jellied bodies, eyes uplifted, lose themselves
In suspended human parts.

Searching blurred heights
I cannot find my waxen limbs.

Years on –
Invasive sun and bubbling tar
Having peeled away the olive trees
The monastery cringes on Moslem ground.
Wonders have ceased there
So I'm told.

But somewhere
Somewhere
My legs must hang.

vi.
On a busy London road, front garden hosed with prayers
My dead mother's giant jasmine coiled in cloisters
Seeds from Cyprus
Collects all passers-by.
They fold into its sweet seducing scent
As if to kiss an icon
Remember how to breathe, hum fragrantly
Flutter like butterflies, rise above themselves.

The head-filling rush of perfume
Like music from other worlds
Can cast a freeing spell
Clear streets of evil
Call the sun to show itself
Make madmen sane.
Even in London.

Even in London
So I'm told.

Initiation at Paphos

The sea rang
Round my seven white years.
I listened to the horizon
Careful
To catch Aphrodite's song.
Perhaps some miracle.

In the distance
Waves pushed the flesh forward.

We had pilgrimaged to this birthplace
To the dry-boned hermit's shrine
Touching holy water
Which had once given voice
To a dumb man.

The flesh was blue-patched
The drowned man floated in

My skin jumped once
Mouth filled with teeth
Fingers pressed my eyes into their sockets.
They towed the cramped weight over rocks.

Identified with a laugh
Bruised and bearded by the sea
He brought relief
        the crazy man, the crazy man
        crossed in love, lost in love
The crazy man wandered villages
Singing poems.

His final poem frothed
Pure white from his tight lips.
They covered him in a blue blanket.

My mother sprinkled holy water over the sea
In my hair

The sea sang.

The Keeper

Eleni
Would not have launched a single ship
Could hardly walk for weight.
Distantly swelling in blurred heat
A swaying blot
Dazed balloon
Hand shielding eyes

Toward the unfamiliar pair
Melting in tarmacadam –
Her grandson
The mother
Deserted by Eleni's wayward son
Across the sea.
He'd wooed and won this wife, Haji-Marie
Left when their child was two.

Five years on, divorced
Haji-Marie brought the boy by train and ship
To meet Yiayia (his Gran)
In Famagusta town.

The taxi-man had queried the address
"You're sure, Madam?"
Then, *"If it's the boy's Yiayia, endaxi I suppose."*

Eleni stepping out of dust
Slipped into human form.
"Mother of God, my grandson!"
Gushed salival blessings
Suffocated his face
Between primped pumpkin-breasts
Pecked daughter-in-law.
Frenetic hugs
Heart-stopping wails to freeze the Styx
Immediate tears, scorching fat-cheeks with guilt.

The taxi-man relieved fell back.

"My stupid son," Eleni trilled, *"my stupid son"*
Urging them toward the house –
A block in length, two floors, four topless towers
"How can I make amends?" she asked the street.

Inside Reception choked with scents, brocaded seats
Into an outdoor Court – a sylvan scene extended
Bursting plants
Ripe fountains
Buoyant balconies.

Eleni gripped grandson's neck to reassure
"One day all this is yours"
His swelling eyes fixing like film
A moon-white buttock at a window tasting air.

Among knocking bamboo
Sharp rhythmic pants
Impossible shrieks, throat-clearing barks of African baboons.
And from the garden corner leaping like gazelles –
An ancient urn lurched into life –
Two naked bodies giving chase between the trees.

The mother crushed his vision to her heated dress
Hedged him in stages to the street.
The house was hollow
Cursed
A ploy
A Kerhane.
Deserved to burn.
Yiayia was Keeper
Queen of bordellos on the wine-dark coast.

The waiting driver
Smiling
Sealed them safe.

Haji-Marie spat thrice, crossed herself
Wrapped a shawl around son's head
Blocked out the shrinking topless towers
Maids in distress

Her offspring's inflamed dreams.

The Dead Poet and Methuses

In Laconia's Spartan land
On the stony beach of Monemvasia
Purple rock where poet Ritsos lies

We were warned.
They warned us

Jellyfish – Methuses
Unfurled
So harmless
Small

Purple eyes

Delighting in cool
Membraneous pulses
Of clear water.

A distant spear-fisher
Helmeted with waterfalls of hair
Bristle-bearded
Grenade-tight as a rock-urchin
Flickered into molecules of light

Raised his melting trident
Like a pen

Encouraging.

The sun
Appeared to push us in among them –

Flared heads on water
Icons
Seething halos of curls
See-through snakes trembling welcomes.

We should have been alarmed.

We floated
Interweaving fluorescent aliens edging closer
Eager fairy rings that
Dragged Time
Down.

Almost regretful, unable to resist
They waved toward rocks
Invited us to spill into their lives

Doorway to other worlds.

Hanging, helpless
We drifted.

The spear-man stroked through waves toward us
Unfolded patches of fire.

A freak cloud leaching sea of colour
Blanketed the methuses
Melted
Closed them out

Allowed Time to surface.

We slipped to solid, safer ground.

Except, carried on heat-haze
The luminous fisher
Filled our shivering places left in water

Dived deep
Tugged by tunnels of sinking light

Floundered into their ring
Mouth circled for air
Swallowed

Such a small methusa.

We watched him switch-blade out of water
Rigid with electricity
Stung to stone.

Later
Far out
The rolling body stole glances from the sun
Seemed to flash a winning wave
Speared the sea with splinters.

Pigeon

Coffee-house drinkers
Always side-stepped Bezouna's bulk
Which grew to fit her name.

She tamed wild roosters, butting goats
Domesticated men

Yet possessed no pricking spurs, blood-red hose, gapped teeth
Wish to shift beyond her perch for other shrines.

Pigeon-plump as her name, Bezouna could not fly
Weighed down with wealth
Breasts cooing pridefully at passers-by
Heart melting at the sight of a child.

Sat like a seal, sweating inside open door
Studied the sun-fried street
Nibbled sugared-almonds from a dish
Fingered her horny feet.

Husband Michaelis, ant of a man
Forever pushing up a twitching shoulder
Fulfilled her every wish
Except a nightly urge to fly
High above the marriage bed
Make children of their own.

Instead, Bezouna kept over-fed chickens in a run
Pigeons in her straw-filled loft
Goats in the yard for Helim cheese.

Forbidden to harm these
The Coffee-house knew
Michaelis would not tempt her wrath
Think of them as food.
Zivania-drunk he joked
"We are all
All preserved lemons."
No one laughed.

Once a day, bouncing pigeons from their perch
Barefoot Bezouna tramped tremors
Through the baking street
Portering pots of lentil soup to Spiros
Her sister's lime-faced runt of a son.
Adopted in her heart, she attempted to entice his love
With pungent home-cooked food.

Told by his mother, act humble, be a surrogate-son
Gain a place in Bezouna's Will
Spiros squeezed rancid smirks onto his lips
Took what he could.
Stole from her purse.

Spiros fell ill. Shivering fits.
Mother blamed the lentil soup
Evil-eye.
Demanded help with doctor's bills.
Bezouna flapped from house to house.

It was Kismet – lemon-faced Spiros died.

Bezouna, broken-winged, withdrew into her home.
Devoured sweet preserves, more almonds, pills
Walnut-stuffed figs, sujuk
Mirroring the moon-struck hills.

Michaelis shrank beneath her bosom, picked his nose.
Received, if someone passed, Bezouna's shrieking slap.
Wore extra-long sleeved shirts to cuff his hands.

So much sweetness
Must have suffused her blood.
The village watched her slip –
Spit at her lodgers, crying "Rape"
Tear Michaelis' smile with ice-picked words
Swear friends were making love to cats…

Kept awake
Michaelis nightly mashed blood-starred mosquitoes
Onto white-washed walls.

Shivering Bezouna, like a fledgling
On nest's edge, fell
Soaked in lava-fired fevers.
Her heart burst
As she grasped at Michaelis' hand.

Finally she flew
With pigeons that Michaelis freed.

He took her place inside their door
Dodging imaginary blows.
Secret twitches see-sawed him to the central step.
Defiant
Sat without a shirt
Nibbled sugared-almonds
Milked his nose

Began to grow.

The Karaghiozi Shadow-Play

The hairless puppet-master revives in the dark
Prefers not to be seen.
Sheds his shame into his one-man show
The twenty characters he speaks.

Appears like a mushroom
In kerosene light by the misty river
Scenting the village square.
Seeming more than he is.
His fungal features rule the dark
Behind the puppets' sheet.

No one calls his name.
Only: *"Karaghiozi, Karaghiozi's come"*
Every midsummer
Crown of the village year,
Folks' island news, cinema, t.v.

Cardboard cut-outs loom on the screen
Like shadow-profiles in a fire-bright cave
Become for all
All the truth there is

Fierce applause, peanut shells, cat-calls
Pepper his sheet.
Barbecued food rushed to clustered tables, loaded seats.
Kebab-smoked flaps of air
Lift his pleased hare-lip like a bridal blush.

He manipulates the hunchback, cuckold, idiot
Fermenting dormant spores
Re-living patterns dried by time

Becomes himself the Karaghioz – 'Black-Eye.'
A simple man
Easily betrayed by a wilful wife.

His bald head boils with horns

Infected by the evil-eye.

With every shadow-shift of lore, he reels folk in

His skewered Karaghiozi breathes into their dreams.
Enchanted, elf-lit men and children
Occupy each others hearts

"Perhaps
Black orbs absorb the evil-eye..."

Husbands touched by shadow-lives
Later share these tales with house-bound wives.

All know the Master's wife had plucked him dry
Stored-away his sight
Seduced the younger brother.

It's said the Master fed them poisoned toadstools
Fried with egg.

Black orbs do absorb
The evil-eye –

Mashallah
Mashallah.

They cheer, cocooned by night
As puppet Karaghiozi beats his wife

Punch after punch.

Never There

Fivos
Simple
Overblown boy
Never caught fire
Since birth never spoke.
"Issue of poetical folk," café-elders sighed
"Suckling mother's milk aged five."

Unschooled – everyday he worked
Unmoved among screaming train-steam
Straw-matted market's Karkashilik –
Scorched songs of cross-legged sellers
Tanging metal-workers
Burdened belches of camel-caravans
Barefoot-blown dust.

Stood silent in black beside the passing track
Features fixed
In bold-type on Kyrenia's purple hills –
Bundle of papers under one arm
Tight fingertips white as wood pulp
Arm a flicking railway signal, rigid headline
Telescoping narratives he could not read

Mutely hawking Father's hand-pressed poems
While the world rushed on –
All Fivos knew – Samson at the mill.

Sliding coins, shifting print tanned his palms.
Days slipped away like flies.

His fickle father trawled mountain villages
Netting news –
Willing widows' preserved fruits
Rhyming events, marriages, baptisms
Revenge killings, runaway lovers
Deaths.

Home only to set his print on paper.
On his wife.

They found Fivos a shoeless, sun-black, widowed bride
With two ragged sons.
(Husband kicked dead by his cow).

The elders drank his wedding dry
Laughed themselves to bed.

Fivos through every edition
Unknowingly sold his own story
Offered up his life.

Winter nights
Stiff as paper
Face a folded grey, sagging out of doorways
Rain soaked through this hamster in its wheel.
The village and their donkeys trampled by.

Like his father
He was never there.

Only in his one room mud home, dimmed in oil
A waiting warmth of wife and sons –
"Again, tell us. Tell us stories."

After onions, black-eyed beans, sour bread
Jezve rolling coffee to a froth
Fivos' face broke
Burnt the room with suns
Began to talk, tongue tapping out –

Mournful
Falling notes of Morning doves

Waking door opening
To a fierce punch of sun

Hunchbacked hills
Shifting shape like wary diplomats

Donkey that shat
On his master's hand

Golden dates –
Busy bunches making honey
Without the help of bees

Molten pomegranates
In a burning bush

Marzipan-bursts
Of sun-ripe oleander

Walking on mirrors –
Beneath a full moon in bubbling rain

Drunken belches of jasmine
On a staggering breeze

Spilt moonlight
Threading milk down a cobbled path
Led by a white cat…

Outside –
Mind corrugated with moments
Fivos waned.

Surrounded by a changing wilderness –
Kept his distance

Liking people too much
To get to know them.

After the Lemons (1969)

At noon
Kyrenia's crescent harbour encloses like a crab
A simmering blue soup of red-sailed caiques
Shivering.
A bloodshot sea.

Feathers of heat lift
Fracturing the Muezzin's call
Ripe figs dropping
Ear-raising howl of the half-blind hound

Mistakenly shot by his master
Who slips over sloped cobbles
Oozing sour wine, salt, Zivania
And bitter
Bitter Lemons.
An ex-freedom fighter – nine years after.

Fried on uneven streets
We seek *Clito's Tavern* and celebrated Clito
Durrell's bosom drinking friend
Their moon-lit bonds baptised by winey promises
Whispers on a breeze, weaving stars, sleepy seas
Sticky breath of jasmine blooms.
That was then.

Clito's, there is no sign.
British bars locked up.
Creaking harbour, cocks crowing
Sweat stealing our sight.

Only the old fighter caught between cobbles
Dares stare in the sun's face.
His stumbling fingers shape our way –
Steep path, warehouse of stone, wood double-entrance.

The screech of sliding iron.
A squinting simpleton peels the doors apart
"You want?"
Behind, steps fall into a bat-black tomb
"Clito Tavern no here!"

We droop.
He sees our faces crease like candlewax.

"Before, yes, yes... You like see? I show."

We sink into the murk, hands tracing air
Advance like lead-men over trip-wire chairs
"Who's there?"
A strange voice falls into our words.
"Beside you – light. Feel along the wall."

The seized switch, clicking pistol-shots
Rebounded by the gloom, crumbles in my hand
Fixes me in Cyclopean guilt.
In a blind-truce we wait as if nursing wounds.

Breaking the dark
The Simpleton lobs back shutters like grenades
Freed light fights its way in –
"You see?"
Dust motes spinning desperately
Flagstone cavern, four straw-pleated chairs.
A seated figure lizard-still, arms feelingly outstretched
Slowly unscrews its head
"Who are you, my friends? I am Clito..."

The simpleton nods.

"Welcome, welcome.
I am sorry,
I am blind, my friends."
Dust freezes in mid-air.
Our hearts weigh down our tongues.

In peacetime, British soldiers, drunk
Aggressive, stamped him blind.
No reason.

"I have written to Durrell –
My good friend.
He will help me.
Doctors, private, you see..."

Hunched over, drawn into a shell
Skull grasped as if avoiding blows
A sea of pain chokes out his thoughts.

The simpleton smirks
Fumbles copy-cat fingers
Around his turnip-head like pincers.
Sign of innocence, betrayed

Cuckold's horns.

The Violinist

Pressed against lime-washed walls
White tables lining the street
Panayiotis – 'Blessed by the Virgin'
Sat alone
Squeezed in pain.
Elongated limbs cramped by wicker chair
Head sunk within a hunched torso
An arthritic daddy-longlegs
Waiting to unfold.

No one used his name
Just *'Violaras – the Violinist'*
'Son of the Violinist'
'Grandson of the Violinist…'
Self-taught.
Blessed with inherited music from the stars.

Villagers usually kept away
He had the means to drive them mad with dance
Make old ones vain
Pierce even the most reluctant
With his sounds.
They believed he had the evil-eye
Spat thrice when he creaked past their door

Yet every wedding begged him play.

This was a time of
Young mens' evening strolls to choose a maid
Sitting outside her open door.
A touch of shadows, lift of female eyes
Midnight shutters fed on nightly serenades.
Marriage Brokers, three day weddings
The hanging out of married sheets.

Rosining his bow, middle of the feast
Violaras would breathe.
Blessed with 'the gift' ignored his pains.
Cheek caressing the violin's hip
Sweaty chin on folded handkerchief
Eyes rolled white, fluttering like breeze-brushed leaves
He listened for secret signs.
Played what was sent into his head.

His sinuous arm stretched notes slow
Onto his strings
Pressed each fret hard until it wailed
Swooped to catch sent-notes, before they left.
Strings found their pitch
Made wedding parties weep
Jerked Violaras to puppet-dance
Grappling the violin
As if holding down a fighting snake
"Yiasou, re-Violara!"

Tips-bowl overflown with coins
Bunched notes thrown at his feet
The street would heave.
Even chickens pecked dancers' shoes
In time to the beat.

Day-break –
Drugged scarecrow steps.
Limp cigarettes on dancer's lips.
Arms flung back, drunk on air.

Violaras could improvise until the end of time.

His time was stopped by travelling youths
Bearing modern magic, which they wound.
They had no muse

Only brittle as biscuit black discs
Spun inside a box
Releasing wondrous, singing souls.

Violaras lost patience waiting *his* muse's clues

Stopped listening
Attempted to compete
Bent to wedding guest requests.

He felt betrayed.
Weddings preferred the youths.

Nobody cared for his soundless screams
Made to a hollow room
Waiting for walls to speak.

Neighbours watched him lose himself
Nurse his violin like a child.

Bereft, he shuffled circles
Pointed his hopeful hand and bow into the ether
Like feelers, tapping blind –

And the village felt relief.
They believed he had the evil-eye
Spat thrice when he creaked past their door.

An English Resurrection

On a sun-grogged island my grandmother lies
Tippling her worry beads…

With midsummer, I escape my trap

The bouzouki's scorpion stings my side
My fingers creak into a dancing stance.

I rack a rose between my lips
And burn amongst the frosted buns
Soak sour tea from china spouts
Whirl manners in a glass

I click the world onto my palms.

Midsummer is *my* rising time.

On a toothless island my grandmother crowed
Cracked into a cavern

Blowflies sizzled, while cicadas split their skin.
Pomegranates bled on jasmine flowers.

Curled around the prickly pears
Crouched on holy ground
I spike stained glass and run
Scuttling the chilled chanting through the cowled arch

Sail smooth as an olive across the sea
Until the knotted handkerchief above my head
Snows
About my face.

Three fingered
My grandmother makes the cross

I have not hanged myself.

Sea Signs

From the cliff-top
I watch a sailboat
Like a whip of wind
A white fleck in a fingernail of blue.

I have a photograph:
I fish off shallow rocks
With a long bamboo.
Waves clash
Spray dots my picture.
In summer I am surrounded by flecks of snow.

Melon seeds and coca-cola cans
Black olives like goat droppings
Collect on the water.
The sea has spread a blue tablecloth
And is having a picnic.

My face is caught in the water.
A small fish wriggles in my eye.

I dive from a caique
And meet myself
On the sea's skin .

The sea closes my mouth
It likes quiet.
I must not shout
I am a guest under its roof.

The fisherman on his boat
Peers into the sea.
I smile, half asleep
Looking up at him.
Slowly rising
My lips touch his cheek.

Underneath
My fingers brush the reef surface.
My eyes reach the reef's shelf
And fall out of my head.

My spear misses the inkfish.
Cut
My feet leak
A wake of red smoke.
From behind its black cloud
The inkfish skids closer.

Under the stained glass surface
Sunlight falls in shafts.
Spread-eagled in this cathedral
I fly over valleys
In spring bloom.

On the sea's marriage bed
Glowing fish thread themselves
Into veils of bright beads.
I kneel in pillows of sand
And they weave a groom's jewels around my head.

The sea has entered my blood
Its minerals live in my bones.
My tears are the salt sea in my eyes
My sweat is the salt sea on my skin.
On the sand's heat
Oceans break from me.
I hear my fathers sing
Like Sirens.

The Drowned

The sea was red.
Copper mines leaked waste into the bay.

The flat sun sat
On the sea's edge burning
The waves away.

On the cliff top
The old woman perched black
Feet clawing the rock
Peering into the sea's blood.

Almonds trickled from her
Fingers into the sea.
The waves were stilled.

Her grandson, a spindle
Of white in the dazzle
Duck-dived through the slave-ship's skull
To see the drowned men.

The old woman scattered pomegranates
On the sea.
There were no drowned men.

Her grandson searched the rib-cage
Time touched his elbow.
Whirlpools sucked hollows
In the surface.

The old woman let wheat with her black shawl
Fall over the sea.
There were no drowned men.

But the sun spat in her eyes.
She hugged herself tight and cawed
Threw raisins at the sun's face.

Her grandson floated into the sun
Mouth open
Head in flames
Flesh covered in copper.

The drowned men had kissed him
Softly

Like kisses from his dead grandmother.

Buttoned-up Shapes

i.
First Cypriot immigrants 1938.
Fifteen bewildered aliens cocooned in London's frozen factories
Struggling to emerge.

Throats clogged with cotton dust
Minds beaten down by indecipherable wireless flutter
Syrup-warmed songs, rattled rag-trade clatter.
Machines
Drilling moving cloth to shape.

Buttoned-up shapes
Immigrants aspire to be.

Nag of thimble-slipped pinpricks *"Neat stitches!*
Neat stitches! Hurry up!"
Snapped threads burning, steam-kissed pressing pads
Sewn-through seeping fingers
"Time! Time! Lots of dresses!
Hurry up!"

In work they are united.

Day's end
Time-Cards punched, wrung back into nightly rain
Anxious to please, mouthing strange words
That mash their teeth
They melt again in parroted confusion

Eggbox shadowed streets, Ration Books
Delicate tea-cups – 'Minding their own'
Fried smiles of tolerance, powdered eggs
Tipped hats of gentle men, offered seats
Queues
Opened doors
Queues
"F – foreigners…!"

Even in sleep
Sore feet cannot cease pressing treadles down.

Weekends dressed in hope
Washed in rainbows in Lyceum Ballroom
London Cypriot Brotherhood –
Warm outposts in the dark
They attempt to float above themselves.

Glitter-balls revolve mirrored fairy dust
Over charmed couples drowned in dreams
Dancing to oblivion the foxtrot, waltz
Tango, quickstep, samba

Pull together meetings of my two makers.

ii.
Conga lines kickstart
Their Lambeth Walks to frenzied Charlestons
In gas-lit attic rooms…

Unready for fatherhood
The male pushes her beneath wailing bombs
To four backstreet abortions.

My mother's screams are air-raid sirens.

I was the fifth little bastard
I somehow slipped through.

Father left when I was two
And I always felt responsible.

iii.
My mother is a demented 92.
Peering at me, sees only her husband.
Even saying his name, so slow
"Har-ra-lam-bos…"
Love congeals her lips.

Richard is here, the Undertaker.
Mother requires her plot bought in advance.
They know each other well.
Lucid talk of flying bombs, a rented Goodge Street flat
Black-Outs
Corseted Jewish landlady keening 'Ave Maria'
To her untuned piano.
Warning sirens
Insomnia in Underground Stations
Dribbled snores, cheesy feet
Bombed buildings, crumpled sounds.
Landlord Lewis, waistcoat and homburg
Ordered home by 'the Missus' to fetch Bruno, the cat.
The 'All-Clear'
Chilled light
Whole streets moved overnight.
Coleslaw at Lyons Corner House
Chaplin flickers in black and white
Competition wins at Ballroom Dancing
Dancing, dancing, bloody dancing…

The inevitable, *"My bloody husband!"*

Ghosts push up like gorse on dried-out moors.

"When I was pregnant with the George
He was kicking, trying to kill the baby."

iv.
I am in the womb
Jarring thuds from outside
Coming in.

I am two
Ride wind-up songs
On our new gramophone placed on floor.
The turntable carries me round and round.

A blurred hulk swats me to the ground
Somersaults the gramophone through open top-floor window
To the communal back-garden four flights below.

I am three
Gripped on stairs.
Peek through bannister rails.
Below, the passage yellowed by open door
Erupts in dust-motes, seagull cries
Clasped figures swimming in distress.
My absent father beats my mother
To a quick divorce.

I am four
Parked in a pushchair outside dress-factory Exit.
Evening in Warren Street, I should be in bed.
Mother waits in shadows.
Pulls father's long-haired mistress down
Rips her breasts with nappy pins.

v.
I sit transfixed.
This is too much to know.

The past
Is the grip of a crocodile
Tail-twisting you deep into the murk.
Letting you up for a last gasp.
Then down again.

Too late
To shake my mother's firm beliefs,
Wake father from the dead.

The past is as it is.

The years – our choice – so laced together
Trip me up.
They took their time.

Truth, is a long while coming.

Antarctica

Snowy Christmas – Lidlington Place
Our Camden attic flat.
Two peeling rooms
Four frosty floors above ruins from German bombs –
Severed dolls houses with hanging bathtubs
Exposed bedrooms
Fractured jungles of wild-dandelion rubble, and putrefied cats.

Isolated by altitude
Crackling blue church-bell clanging sky
We float in the coal-fired sitting-room, which is our bedroom.
The war is over.
And my father left us.

Baby gas-incubator discarded in the coal-cupboard
(I am 4 years old)
I spin in a revolving concertina of beds and sofa
Legs dangling high off the floor
Body clutched desperately tight
Waltzing my mother cheek to cheek

Able, like the tree's cardboard star, to glimpse
Above oak chest-of-drawers
And wind-up gramophone –
Creaking 78 times to the minute a Greek lament –
The consoling eyes of Scott hanging on our wall
Making his last freezing camp in desolate Antarctica
A whirling wilderness, dervish-devils of snow.

My mother hums to the song of deserted love
Her tears seal our faces.
Just us.

I am the short straw
Sucking down cold sorrow

Never to celebrate Christmas.

Fading

My mother believes I am my father
Yet sharply raps on window-glass
Seeking help from the street.
"I am locked in the Greek Church," she wails.

An attempt at reason
All I can do.
"This is your room," I explain.
"Look on the wall, a photograph of your mother, your son."

She drops into her seat.
"I know, I know," she agrees.
"But why am I in this church?"

Islands

The World is troubled
With a lack of looking.
I sing my songs.
The World sleeps.

I see the sky reflected in my teacup.
I move the cup
And tilt the sky.

The flying crane is shadowed
On the mud wall.
My shadow touches his
And I ride the bird.

The stars are mirrored in a pool
Of rain.
With my hand I scoop up the water.
I have a handful of stars.

I grasp the branch of a tree.
The wind blows
And the tree shakes my hand.

The moon shimmers on my glass of cognac.
I drink
And taste the moon.

I climb a fig tree and look down.
The earth has fallen.

My mother's face appears
On the surface of an olive.
I split the olive
And scar my mother's face.

All the world
All the world pours in at my barred window.
I lower my lids
And dam the floods.

Footnotes

Alien Light
Lapithos: A lush mountain village in Cyprus sweeping down to the sea. Now on the Turkish side and known as Lapta.
Xenofos: The name means 'alien, strange, or foreign light.' This was my maternal Great-Uncle.
Weddings: were traditionally a three day celebration.
Omorpho horko: 'beautiful village' – the derivation of Morphou.

Prickly Pears
Vrakka: a loose-fitting black cotton wrap reaching down to the knee, fashioned into trousers. Usually worn with knee-high leather boots beneath.
Baboutso-siga: Prickly Pears. Literally translated as 'Shoe-figs'.

The Schoolmaster
Yiorgos with a soft 'g' means, 'Cultivator of land'. This was my paternal grandfather after whom I was named.
Okes were a Turkish weight of about 1.3kg used in Cyprus in the past.

Evil Eyes
"The dribbling one": Her real name was Maria, but known as Katchara because of the noise (Katcharizi) she made bursting unannounced into peoples' houses and cursing them.
The Broker: Marriage brokers were employed to arrange suitable matches when no suitors showed interest.
Han: A Caravanserai (resting place for travelling traders and their animals). Used as a derogatory term among Cypriots when house doors are left open.

Ourania
Ourania is the feminine of Ouranos – the general term for 'sky'.
Ourania Atalyani was my second cousin. My mother and I were the only members of the family to accept her.

Ioulia and Francos
Francos (Christos Francos) was my maternal grandfather.
Lefkara village was renowned for its delicate crochet-work. Having now become part of the northern Turkish sector and abandoned by its original inhabitants, the crochet-work from this village has become a rarity and so luxuriously expensive.
Morphou was an important agricultural village, also now in the north of the island.
Christian Haj: Greek Orthodox pilgrims, as a sign of religious devotion (mirroring the Moslem Haj to Mecca) visit the Christian holy sites in Jerusalem, are re-baptised in the River Jordan, and to mark the occasion are granted use of the prefix, 'Haji'.
Little red men: This prophesy was specifically referring to a Chinese race of the future.

So I'm Told

Andreas The Apostle: Brother of St. Peter and one of the 12 Apostles personally appointed by Christ. On a return journey to his home in Palestine, the Apostle's ship docked in the Karpaz area of Cyprus in search of water. When he walked onto the land, a spring gushed from below his feet. The blind Captain drank the water and his sight was miraculously restored. This became a major pilgrimage site for the Greek-Orthodox community.

Olive-leaves: The smoke of burnt olive-leaves, like church incense, is meant to dispel evil. N. American Indians also used a particular smoke to cleanse their auras.

Watery gap: Before the Channel Tunnel and cheap air-flights, the most economical way to reach Cyprus was to cross the Channel by Ferry, train to Naples, Genoa or Venice and then third class berth on a Passenger-Ship.

Panhandle-tip: How the Karpaz peninsula of Cyprus, like a 'pointing finger', is commonly described. The Monastery of Andreas the Apostle is situated on its very edge.

Pastelli/Soujouko: The first was a hard, sweet disc made from carob syrup, much like today's 'Crunchie'. The second was made by dripping boiled grape-must down string that threaded through almonds, layer by layer, until it hardened into a sweet, rubbery sausage.

Invasive sun/Moslem ground: 1974 Turkish troops landed in Cyprus and laid claim to the northern part of the island, which is gradually being built-up with Golf-Course, Boat-Marina and numerous Villa developments. Most developments seem to have no planning strategy, and remain unchecked by officialdom.

The Keeper

Eleni: My paternal grandmother.

Endaxi: Commonly used Greek word meaning, 'Alright' or 'Okay'.

Styx: In Greek mythology the River Styx existed as a watery dividing line between mortal life and the Underworld (Hades).

Kerhane: A Turkish word (commonly used in Cyprus) for 'Brothel'.

Spat thrice: Spitting three times in the direction of a suspect person, or place, averts evil.

The Dead Poet and Methuses

Methuses: The Greek name for Jellyfish. In English – Medusas.

Monemvasia: A fortified town on a cyclamen-covered rock in the Laconian area of the Peloponnese – founded AD 585. Used to be known for its production of Malvasia (Malmsey) wine.

Ritsos: Yiannis Ritsos, a major 20th Century Greek dissident poet, who was jailed and whose poetry was banned in Greece until 1972. Born and buried in Monemvasia.

Other worlds: Ancient Greeks believed there were shafts that led to the Underworld (Hades). One such renowned site, locals claim, still exists on the southernmost tip of the Laconian middle-finger of the Peloponnese at Marmari, Cape Taineron.

Pigeon

Bezouna: The Cypriot name literally translates as 'female pigeon' but colloquially has also come to mean a large, masculine, dominant woman. Much as 'the cock of the roost' is applied to dominant females in Britain. A classic literary example being the Wife of Bath on pilgrimage to Canterbury. She wears spurs, bright red hose and is gap toothed, which signifies dominance and lasciviousness, according to Chaucer.

Helim: (Or Halloumi) A salty, rubbery goat's milk cheese. Now mass-produced from ewes' and cows' milk.

Zivania: A clear spirit from grape-leavings after wine-making.

Preserves: Villagers boil-up and preserve in syrup orange-peel, aubergine, water-melon peel, ground almonds, fresh walnuts in their green skins etc. Guests are traditionally welcomed with these sweet offerings, accompanied by a glass of water.

Sujuk: A 4-foot long string threaded with almonds is dipped into heated grape-syrup, which has been thickened with a little flour. This is hung up to harden and the process repeated until a rubbery rope of approximately an inch in diameter is created.

Mosquitos: Mosquito-borne malaria was prevalent in Cyprus until 1952. A British eradication project (1945-1952) utilised the planting of thirsty eucalyptus trees to drain swampy areas, so drying-up mosquito breeding grounds.

The Karaghiozi Shadow-Play

Karaghioz: The name of the main puppet-character, the trickster, translates as 'Black Eye' in Turkish.

Karaghiozi is the Greek way of pronouncing the word and it has gradually become to mean 'Clown'. It is often used as an insult. A descendant of the ancient shadow-puppets of the orient through the Byzantine and Ottoman empires. Some say Karaghioz originated in China. It is a precursor of the masked Italian Commedia dell'arte, and of Punch and Judy. The many stories in Karaghioz (originally based on fact) though formulaic, nevertheless allow the puppeteer to devise improvisational strands and even to create his own original tale.

Mashallah: When praising or complimenting a person, it is customary to conclude with "Mashallah, Mashallah" (God has willed it) in order to clarify the selfless and innocent intention behind the compliment and so guard against the person being touched by the 'evil-eye' (jealous or malevolent thought). Alternately, the person complimented can, on departing, turn and spit three times over their shoulder to repel 'the eye,' or have on their person a blue 'evil-eye bead'.

Never There

Fivos: This Greek name derives from Phoebus (Apollo the sun-god).

Steam-train: There was a simple steam-train operating in Cyprus until 1952. From its base in Nicosia it travelled to all the major towns. The steam engine still exists and is displayed in the municipal gardens of Morphou (now renamed Guzelyurt).

Karkashilik: A Turkish word commonly used in Cyprus to describe 'a hullabaloo'.
Jezve: Turkish word for a long-handled metal utensil used to boil Turkish coffee to a froth.
Diplomat: The word is Greek and literally translates as 'double-eyed' or in other words, 'two-faced'.
Cobbled path: This is an existing Crusader path leading uphill to the village of Bellapais and its ancient Abbey, where the writer Lawrence Durrell lived for a time and wrote about in his book, 'Bitter Lemons'.

After the Lemons
Durrell (Lawrence) lived in Cyprus 1953 – 1956. This was during the Cypriot struggle for independence from Britain. He bought a house in the village of Bellapais, Kyrenia, taught English in Nicosia and wrote a book based on his experiences entitled, 'Bitter Lemons.' Clito is one of the main characters.
Zivania: A clear spirit from macerated grape-skins, after wine has been distilled.

The Violinist
Weddings: Receptions were usually a three day affair. Whole streets were blocked off with oil drums and tables laid out with food and copious alcohol. An opportunity for the parents of the bride to display their wealth.
Yiasou: 'To your health.' Also used as a greeting.

The Drowned
The Greek Orthodox faith celebrates an Anniversary of The Dead. Each year a mixture of boiled wheat, pomegranates, raisins and almonds is presented to the church by relatives who wish to have the names of the dead remembered during this special service. The gesture also serves as an offering to appease the dead.